Nursing Home Survival Manual

By

A. Frank Rushton, PhD

Alternative Book Press
2 Timber Lane
Suite 301
Marlboro, NJ 07746
www.alternativebookpress.com

2014 Paperback Edition
Copyright 2013 © A. Frank Rushton

Cover Illustration by Alternative Book Press
Book Design by Alternative Book Press
All rights reserved
Published in the United States of America by Alternative Book Press

Originally published in electronic form in the United States by Alternative Book Press
Library of Congress Cataloging-in-Publication Data

A. Frank, Rushton, [date]
Nursing Home Survival Manual/ by A. Frank, Rushton.—1st ed.
p. cm.
1. Non-Fiction (Non-Fiction). I Title.
AG2-600.R87N877   2013
001—dc23
2013957086

ISBN 978-1-940122-08-3
Printed in the United States of America
10 9 8 7 6 5 4 3 2 1

From the Author:

My Dedication:

My road to a more meaningful life was inspired by my late wife, LeJean Alexander Rushton, and by my Major Professor at Florida State University, Dr. Robert Branson. In preparation of this book, my very close friend and colleague, John Andrews, generously offered his time and energies as editor and counsel. My friends and cousins, Betty Godwin, Miranda Lotz, and Jenny Huffaker have given immeasurable support and caring in the considerable adjustment to nursing home life. Good people, I love you all.

A. Frank Rushton

Throughout this manual we have provided you with blank pages so that you may write notes as the Author will instruct. This enables you to take this book with you

Table of Contents:

Preface

You may remember a pleading parent saying: "Please don't ever put me in a nursing home." Or: "I'd rather die than be in a nursing home." Yet your parent's condition left no choice. What were you to do?

Life's pace moves us on. One sad day my beloved wife's health had deteriorated to a point from which I could no longer care for her. It was simply not possible. Over a prolonged period of years I had been her sole caregiver. Now the time had come. Our physician tactfully explained to her why this step was necessary. I do not remember LeJean having any negative response.

Now, in your life the unthinkable has begun to appear. Your own worsening health seems to be reaching the dreaded point where you will require admission to a nursing home. You resist. You may say something like this to family members: "Give me a chance. Please believe that I can live on my own." Those were my precise words.

Or you may be reaching a decision on behalf of a beloved family member who can no longer care, or perhaps even think, for herself or himself. Regardless of the situation in which you find yourself, I respectfully ask that you walk with me through a series of important steps. You will learn something about what to do when facing a nursing home decision, as well as coping with events which will follow. Living in a nursing home does not mean the end of meaningful living. But it can and must set you on a journey to find a new way of

doing it.

Chapter One - First Steps

The Journey Begins

An Important Personal Note: This is personal for me, because I have followed the path to be described, and it is important for me as a person to share this experience. Hopefully reading these pages will make it easier for each of you just starting the journey. On the other hand, you may be a family member or close friend of a person in need of nursing home services. For me, that keeps the matter personal. My hope is that these words will make the path to be trod significantly easier to follow.

I will discuss admittance to and residence in a nursing home. If a person is, even for the most part, in full possession of his or her mental abilities, he or she may be taking that step as an individual, or together with family members.

Hopefully this book will also be helpful to the family of the person no longer able to think as an individual. This would be with regard to observations and facts about the nursing home experience applicable to all patients.

Do not avoid thinking of

anything you find unpleasant or even overwhelming. In the beginning of this process, it will probably be wise to seek the help of many opinions.

Selecting the Nursing Home

Here's something you should keep burning in the forefront of your consciousness: All nursing homes are not alike. You may be surprised at the differences you
find when you begin your walking tours.

Begin With These Steps: By appointment visit your own county or area welfare or aging office. It may take a little digging to determine the mission and name of the organization or organizations you should visit. Insist on talking to the person in charge of the program in which you are interested. **Do not be deterred**.

Not all counties may be well staffed or funded for their mission, or perhaps they may not address the mission at all. My own county has a Department on Aging. Check around, and, if necessary, go to the nearest metropolitan agency you find.

After you have read all the materials you have acquired,

and talked to knowledgeable people you have identified, you should have excluded some unlikely prospects. As well, you will now have a list of prospects to visit on your own walking tour.

Tip: You will find, as is likely, that adjusting to the nursing home reality is a somewhat slow, evolving process: Ask family members whose judgment you respect to make an initial walking tour for you.

With some of the information gained from their efforts, you will probably be more comfortable as you look into the situation. Again, in my own case, this turned out to be true.

However the walking tour list is developed, the tour must be made. We now turn to criteria by which you should be guided.

As you read what follows, you will encounter an occasional cautionary note about signs indicating possible negative things to be avoided.

Walking Tour

Tip: Be sure to acquire a small, easily managed notebook before visiting a nursing facility. You may think you will remember all important details. Trust me, you won't. Take two writing instruments, pen or pencil, in case the first one fails.

What follows will apply to each nursing facility visited. If you are fortunate you will find a home which meets or exceeds the criteria we identify. The results of your decision process should satisfy as much as possible all those criteria immediately concerned. Good luck.

NOTES

The Administrator's Briefing

You have now made an appointment to see a home. You must, quite politely of course, insist on an interview with the Administrator, privately, in his or her office.

Listen to the Administrator's comments, which should in effect be a sort of briefing. We will assume that this is a privately owned, for profit, facility. Be sure to make notes. At the time you may feel that you will remember key points. Given the stress of the moment you probably will not.

Tip: Make those notes.

NOTES

If the following questions are not answered, then ask them. Here they are:

1. Has the facility been certified or rated recently by any agency?

You should be told the name of the agency, and the Rating made

2. Who owns the facility?

3. What persons comprise the top administrative staff?

What are their titles, duties, and relationship, if any, to ownership?

4. What departments or sections make up the facility,

and who is in charge of each section? Of course, there will and must be a kitchen staff. The facility should provide for an Activities Department, under an Activities Director, and a Physical Therapy/Occupational Therapy Department, under a Director of highest qualifications. There must be an equally qualified Social Worker.

5. Who provides medical care and treatment for the facility's residents, and on what basis or schedule?

Remember, make notes. You'll need them when later considering your tour, and of

course in reaching
conclusions.

NOTES

Tip: If the facility's primary care physician is not known to you, or known in the community, you may want to ask about his training and his practice. Of course this information may be found elsewhere.

Be sure to continue the interview with the Administrator until you are satisfied with the nature and completeness of the information you have obtained.

You are almost ready for your tour, which must and will be offered you. Do not allow the tour to take place until you have had that comprehensive

interview or discussion with
the administrator. He or she
must have been willing to
answer your questions.

The tour will be conducted by the Administrator, or by some key person assigned to the task. What follows now is a list of the areas {for lack of a better name} you should ask to see.

There may be some personal suggestions, given that I am presently a resident in a highly rated nursing home. I shall not identify that home in this book.

If you find that the nursing home you are touring lacks any of the facilities or staff members I mention, leave the tour as quickly and as comfortably as possible, and cross that facility off your list.

You must insist, if necessary, on seeing all of them.

Hopefully, you will find at least one nursing home up to standard in your area. The available options in that case may well depend on personal or family resources, commitments, and time and expense associated with travel.

Now, let us turn to the areas or departments which should be on your list. The person conducting your tour will probably point out features which the nursing facility considers impressive. Just be sure your tour includes everything mentioned here.

We shall begin with the residential halls, or corridors. They are likely to be numbered or designated in some way. Then we'll go on to other essential areas.

As previously indicated, the assumption in writing this book is that you {or your loved one's family} will, with your escort, be strolling the halls in a privately owned, for profit, Medicaid/Medicare accepting facility.

While much of the information here will be useful in evaluating other types of facilities, we do not refer to a home which provides guaranteed care through various stages of health. In such places you may be required to pay a hefty entrance fee.

We are now ready to begin the tour. Let us proceed.

The Tour

Here is an important note: As you tour the building, on every step of the way, it should pass the Smell Test.

Yes, the Smell Test. Odors should not be detectable, especially those having to do with fecal matter as you walk the residential corridors of the facility. Such odors should not be present. You {or your loved one} will only wish to live in a facility where cleanliness holds an extremely high priority. Pleasant living to the greatest extent possible in a nursing facility is only possible when that priority is met.

Area 1 - The Residential Halls

As you stroll the halls, you will probably find that some of the rooms' doors are open and some of them are closed.

If a resident has a "friendly" expression on his or her face, speak to them. If they seem to want to talk a bit, take the moment to do so. It may bring a little happiness to the resident and a partial impression of the home to you. If the resident is really friendly, you may feel that you can ask to see the room. Most of the rooms will be semi-private, and some will be private.

Bear in mind that many of the residents, or perhaps most of them, may have lost full mental acuity. This is a layperson's opinion, and probably a correct one. Otherwise, it would not be a nursing home; it would be a retirement community.

You may want to ask your tour guide to show you both a semi-private and a private room, even if unoccupied. By all means, inspect at least two toilets. They should be extremely clean. Bear in mind that Smell Test.

NOTES

Area 2 - The Shower Room

"What's this?" you say. "A shower room?" you ask. The answer is, given that all residents have limited abilities, there must be a facility in which all needs can be met.

You may expect it to be very, very clean. There will be a large tiled room with a therapeutic tub, a shower stall, and a washbasin with a mirror. Your CNA {Certified Nursing Assistant} will assist your personal needs.

Something to keep in mind: Taking a shower in a large, clean room, with a qualified person to assist you, will require adjustment and acceptance on your part, and that will take time. Try to be as gracious as possible.

A personal aside, probably mostly of interest to me: I found the evenly lit shower room mirror to be the best place to check the appearance of my cherished, albeit uneven, mustache.

To emphasize, before leaving this area, the standard is absolute, unvarying cleanliness. Let us say it again, "absolute unvarying cleanliness."

Before leaving, ask your escort

any questions you may have about equipment you notice in the Shower Room. Just remember, the more you ask, throughout your tour, the more you will know, and the more you know, the better qualified you will be able to make a decision as to whether this facility is for you, or for your loved one, as the case may be.

NOTES

Area 3 - The Physical Therapy Facility

This facility may be called something similar, or even quite different. Its purpose is to provide Physical and occupational therapy needed by and for each individual patient.

This treatment may be specified by medical personal responsible for the wellness of the facility's residents, or by someone else.

The Director of this facility must be highly qualified. What is his title? What are his academic qualifications? And what are the key elements of his career, of his experience? If you ask for proof of these qualifications, someone should be willing to provide it, or at the very least, to assist you in obtaining the information. Ask, ask, ask, until you are satisfied.

There is much to know. Does the facility employ both physical therapists and occupational therapists? What does each of the specialties do?

Again, ask about qualifications, and let it be known that should you want proof, you will expect it to be provided. Or, at the least, where may you turn for this information? In a good facility, this last quest may not be necessary.

Once again, do not be hesitant. You have a right to this information. You, or if you are a loved one's family or family member, will need it in making a decision.

Oh, by the way, I will get around to *Survival* In A Nursing Home. But first, that nursing home must be selected!

NOTES

Area 4 - Kitchen and Dining Room

You will probably be escorted through the dining room on your way to the kitchen. Your escort may have some comments about the dining room; just suggest you would first like to see the kitchen, then return to the dining room.

This is quite reasonable, of course. If you find the kitchen below standard, you most certainly would not wish to eat, or to have someone you love eat, in the dining room, no matter how pleasant.

Because of variation in size or scope, I will offer only general comments or suggestions. The first would apply to any kitchen, anywhere.

The kitchen must be uniformly clean. Every wall, all of the floor, every pot and pan, every plan, every instrument or utensil, in short everything, must be clean to a very high standard.

The Health Department's Inspection rating should be prominently posted, and it should be high indeed. Here's a thought: It would probably be a good idea to call the Health Department making the facility's rating, and asking for an explanation of that rating.

You will probably be introduced to the person in charge of the kitchen. If not, then ask to meet that person. Talk to every person on duty in the kitchen at the time of your visit. Each should be open and friendly, willingly answering any question about their duties.

Later in this book there will be a section on "Personal Caregivers," meaning the nurses and CNAs {remember, Certified Nursing Assistant} having the responsibility for your care, or that of your family member, twenty-four hours a day, seven days of the week. In the above, we have restricted the discussion to those working in the kitchen.

Having completed the kitchen portion of our inspection tour, we turn now to the dining room. Its requirements may be summarize briefly and concisely: The dining room simply must be clean, clean, clean. It should also be attractive.

Since the meaning of "attractive" will likely vary between persons, you will probably be able to rather quickly form your own opinion.

As far as the kitchen and

dining room are concerned, here's a last important word. Do not, repeat do not, expect the food served to be comparable to that served at an upscale gourmet restaurant. Lets assume that we are likely looking over a privately owned, for profit facility.

The profit margin may not be great, meaning that you will not have been likely to meet a Chef or Registered Dietitian. There will be diabetic needs to be considered, as well as those of patients with sensitive digestive systems.

Nevertheless, balanced meals

should be available. All of that being said, it is time to move on.

NOTES

Area 5 - The Activities Room

For starters, there should be an Activities Room. There should be an Activities Room and an Activities Director. The lack of such a "combined" resource should be a warning sign. You should discuss with the Activities Director all of the programs and activities she plans, arranges, and supervises. Does she have a stipulated budget within which she must meet her responsibilities? Which duties are delegated to the Assistant Director?

You should find that you have at least an initial impression of whether the Activities Director is a competent and caring person. In this you may be wrong, but at least you should have had time in which to reach some sort of conclusion.

Tip: Ask enough questions to determine whether management adequately supports the Activities Department

NOTES

Nursing Home Survival

We have at last arrived at the "Survival" portion of this Nursing Home Survival Manual. Up till now, we have discussed matters which must occur to make what we are going to say relevant.

There will be no attempt to discuss in detail the procedures you must undergo, or the sequence in which they will occur.

It stands to reason that there must be tests and measurements taken to obtain information needed to give you proper care, mostly of a medical nature. Suffice to say, these will occur in the early days.

We will discuss how to deal with the overriding new reality: You are now in a nursing home. Unless you are temporarily there for assistance in recovering from an auto accident or some other hurtful occasion, you will be in a nursing home. To repeat, you will be in a nursing home. Always. This means you will have a lot of adjusting to do. So, lets get on with it.

Chapter Two - Your New Path
First Day

Your stay in a nursing home must be paid for by someone, or some "thing," meaning a likely combination of government agencies. The person managing your financial affairs will have worked this out with the facility's business office, or will be in the process of doing so. The Welfare Worker will likely have assistance to offer.

If we assume that as you read these words, you are a person in possession of mental acuity {or whatever term you may prefer}, he or she will explain things to you as they occur.

In all likelihood, you will have given to him or her your power of attorney. This is something else to which you must adjust, and which will be again mentioned as we proceed.

Unless arrangements have been made, by whatever means, for you to occupy a private room, you will have been assigned to semi-private housing. Assignment to a semi-private room means you will be sharing that room with another person. More about that in a moment.

So, here you are, in bed at last.

During the day, things have gone by in a whir, and you may be pardoned if you are in some kind of daze, that is to say a mentality exemplified by the question, "What am I doing here?"

Your evening meal has been served, and you will have been assisted in your bedtime rituals, and even in getting in bed, by the CNA. We will discuss this person, usually a "she," but quite possibly a "he," when we consider "Your Caregivers."

Tip: Early in your residence at a nursing facility, or even prior to admission, consider acquisition of a "Grabber," sometimes also called a "Reacher." As you probably know, this is a simple device with a handle and trigger or pull lever at one end, and an arrangement at the other which permits you to "grab" or pick up things.

You may drop something on the floor, or something may be just out of reach. This could be, for example, on your bedside table. I have found the Grabber to be one of the most useful gadgets I have ever owned.

Note that I said "consider acquisition" rather than "buy." It may be that your facility will provide one without charge. Ask your Director of Nursing.

So now, nighttime lighting will have been adjusted. You will almost certainly be quite tired, and probably well stressed. Yet, this is your first opportunity to think seriously about your situation, without other interruptions or distractions.

Now, back to matters at hand: You will need many "think times," so this one is just a start, albeit a very important one. During this time, here are some things you should consider, important things. Your status, your situation, the reality of it, should come first. You are in a nursing home. To repeat, you are in a nursing home. As much as you may resist the thought, once again, you are in a nursing home.

Discounting the possible exception we have already mentioned, you are likely in a nursing home for the rest of your life. Overwhelming? Of course it is. Are you resenting it? Most likely you are. Do you dislike the requirement that you must have others to assist you in previously normal or routine functions? Of course you do.

Nevertheless, this is and will be the reality. You will not be able to have your brain process it, and your conscious mind to accept it, in a short period of time.

There may be moments for the rest of your life when you resist this presently new reality. But you must work hard, very hard to accept that it is indeed, real: "I am in a nursing home." But you must start, and start tonight.

Here's another trait of nursing home life which may require some adjustment: Taking a shower, to some extent going to the toilet, continuous checking of blood pressure and body temperature, are all functions which will now be monitored.

There may be some variation from resident to resident. And, all of this may seem to you or your loved one to be an invasion of privacy. And, to some extent it is. But it is necessary, to preserve your health as much as possible, and to complete with regulations put in place to safeguard patient well being. I advise accepting this part of your new reality, so you can continue with the adjustment process you must undergo.

You will have met your new roommate, but not yet for a considerable period of time. He, or she, will not, repeat not, share your views and likings in every way. Perhaps the two of you may agree on little, or perhaps with regard to virtually nothing.

What is that I hear you saying? You don't like this. You don't like having personal decisions affected, perhaps even changed, by another individual. Of course you don't.

Neither did I. But the reality meant I had to begin the process, and your reality will enforce your new situation as well.

This adjustment is intertwined with your acceptance of the nursing home reality. And oh yes, it may be very difficult indeed.

Allow me to cite my personal experience. I should explain that over a period of time, repeated falls required temporary admission with a view toward my gaining self-sufficiency.

Finally, it became obvious that for various reasons, I lacked the equilibrium to live on my own. So began what I may call my "permanent residency period."

I was fortunate in that a space was open for which I qualified, a space in this highly rated facility. This was my start.

Now, let's get back to the steps in your process of adjustment.

We have now arrived at the Survival Guide in this book's title, which quite possibly led you to buy it in the first place.

We will number these steps in

your process of adjustment, of your survival. But first, what is now meant by "survival?"

We are here speaking of your survival as an individual, as essentially the person you have been for a very long time, in every way other than your physical limitations.

This is very, very important. Because, you see, you will have a choice. That choice is to keep your personhood, and build on it, or simply roll over, indulge in self-pity, and do nothing.

Now we are going to stop, recapitulate a bit, and move

on. We mentioned that we were going to explain things in numbered steps.

Tip: Remember to keep using and using that small, pocket-sized, notebook. Later, you may be surprised at how useful your notes have become.

Once again, the adjustments we'll be discussing are not immediately or rapidly accomplished. So cut yourself some slack, just be sure to keep self-pity out of the process. Let's get on with those numbered steps. And, remember, as days and months pass, you will be working on more than one numbered step at a time.

Step No. 1 - Acceptance of My New Reality

Of course we still mean acceptance of your new and likely status as a nursing home resident. Do not spend your time denying it, or contemplating unrealistic steps to change it. That is, unless you are the temporary customer here for physical rehabilitation.

Tip: Now would be a good time to an entry in your notebook: "Step No. 1 - Acceptance of My New Reality." Remember, this is going to be a long-term process.

NOTES

Step No. 2 - Adjusting to My New Roommate

So far, we have mentioned this only briefly. Now is time to face it up front, and think about doing it.

There will be differences of course. As to some of them, you may be able to give and accept your roommate's preferences by making your own adjustment to them. There will likely be preferences or behavior where you must simply stand your ground.

Go ahead and write in that notebook: "Step No. 2 - Adjusting to Roommate?"

Here are some examples where adjustments may be made, or ground held:

One of my roommates wanted his bed lamp "on" throughout the night. Even with the curtain drawn between us, his lamp emitted a considerable amount of light. I closed my eyes and made the adjustment. Of course, I didn't much like it, but I did get the sleep I needed.

This gentleman didn't seem to like television sound on past what I considered a too-early hour. I'm a "night person," having been so for a long time. So I kept the TV set on until

10:00P, while being careful to keep the sound at a moderate level.

Another roommate was a rabid sports fan. I am not, having only a limited interest in college football. This person had lived for golf and for basketball.

On some nights when the extra channels he had ordered were having technical difficulty, I made my TV set available. Although we were unlikely to ever become close friends, he did come to see me after I had changed rooms. To digress only briefly, I had an opportunity to take a private room, thus explaining the change.

The mutual adjustment between two roommates can take a rather long time. Or it may be possible that in some ways the relationship can progress in a surprisingly rapid fashion. You will just have to see.

Tip: You will become aware of disturbing or irritating behavior on the part of residents other than your roommate. "Turn it off," for there is nothing you can do about the matter. Trained staff will deal with such things.

Before moving on, there is one

"general adjustment you will have to make. The difficulty of making it will of course vary from person to person.

The majority of a facility's population will with virtual certainty be less fortunate people with varying degrees of mental impairment. If you are of what is popularly called "sound mind," you will just have to learn how to handle it.

Many of these folks are sufficiently "with it" to permit the forming of relationships. Others are not. Give yourself time, for you will learn to live in, and interact with, this environment.

We will soon come to the next step in your adjustment, or survival process. Please remember that in our context, "survival" means survival of your personhood, of you, as essentially the person you have always been.

NOTES

Your Caregivers

As previously promised, it is now time to discuss your caregivers. We must consider the vital interaction between you and these professionals.

You will inevitably find yourself interacting with caregivers during the rest of your life at the nursing facility. Interacting well is a major part of your survival experience and strategy. We will try to be helpful in this respect because, please remember, we are talking about your survival as a person, the product of your life experiences.

But first let us turn our attention to identifying the professions or jobs of caregivers, and in some general sense, their duties.

Basically, your caregivers include three groups of people: Medical, that is physicians {MD} and Physicians' Assistants-Certified {PA-C}; Nurses, both Licensed Practical Nurses {LPN} and Registered Nurses {RN}; and Certified Nursing Assistants {CNA}.

In these discussions, it should be pointed out, we are working in the context of a highly rated facility.

The fact that you're reading these pages suggests that you, a potential resident or family member, are intelligent and responsible, and therefore likely to be interested only in such a facility.

Physicians

Let's talk about physicians first. You may have concluded that if the facility has no permanent, ongoing arrangement for providing medical care to patients, you want no part of it. And you would be right.

When a situation or condition

arises requiring medical care, there should be a recognized and authorized means of obtaining that care.

A Word of Caution: I have made no survey of any kind regarding the various systems in any area, let alone all. Such a project would be enormously difficult and time consuming, not to mention the requirement for expensive personnel.

I am however, familiar with one model that seems to work reasonably well. This is the structure in place at the facility where I live. Here, a locally recognized physician is on call a certain day of the week, and his associate, a Physician's Assistant, is available on another day. Nurses on the floors can access their help at any time.

There will be no identification of this facility. To provide that information would be, in some sense, to change this survival guide into a promotional piece for one facility. Such is not my intention.

The Physician: Now let's talk about the primary member of the facility's medical care team. "Primary" is the appropriate word here, because of the chosen physician's central role in your medical care.

He will likely be a local practitioner of high repute. This physician's work at the facility will, with virtual certainly, be only a part of his practice. We could not reasonably expect the situation to be otherwise.

As in the example, the "model," with which I am familiar, there will likely be specified days on which he, or his assistant, will be in attendance.

In addition, he will always be available to nurses at the facility, so that when questions of a particular nature arise with regard to a given patient, they will be answered in a prompt and responsible time.

Lets talk for a moment about the Physician's Assistant. He, or she, will be a person commonly referred to as a "PA," or "PA-C." PA-C simply stands for "Physician's Assistant-Certified." What does that term mean? The term refers to a person highly trained in medical skills, although not qualified to be an MD, or Doctor of Medicine.

What must a person do to quality as a "Physician's Assistant-Certified?" Although I have long been impressed by the competence and sensitivity of "PAs" in various practices, I did not really know. So, I did what you can do if you have a computer, I went online to find an answer.

My source is Wikipedia, the free online encyclopedia. Here is what Wikipedia says: "A physician assistant {PA} is a healthcare professional who is trained to practice medicine as part of a team with physicians. Specifically, under the direction and supervision of attending physicians."

Wikipedia continues: "Physician assistants are concerned with preventing and treating human illness and injury by providing a broad range of health care services under the direction of a physician or surgeon."

Here in the United States a graduate from an accredited PA program must pass a National Certifying Exam before becoming a PA-C. All states require this certification. So, you see, as a patient or family member you may have confidence in the diagnosis or treatments from a Physicians' Assistant-Certified.

You may find yourself in contact with a Physician or Physician's Assistant with regard to medical diagnoses or treatment. There are also two occupations providing nursing care.

Please be patient, we will soon arrive at the point of discussing interaction with all these people, as part of your Nursing Home Survival Guide, or perhaps better said,
your strategy.

You will encounter two categories, or professions, of nurses. One is the "LPN," or Licenses Practical Nurse. The other is the "RN," or Registered Nurse. In the states of Texas and California, the former is known as a Licensed Vocational Nurse, or "LVN."

Generally speaking, one can become a Licensed Practical Nurse with one year of training. To become a Registered Nurse, it is necessary to hold a two-year degree.

If the would-be nurse wants to hold a four-year degree, or baccalaureate, another two years of study is required. Either category of nurse is equipped to provide you with competent professional care.

There is one more category, of professional caregiver whom you will encounter as a nursing home patient or, if you like, resident. This is the Certified Nursing Assistant, usually referred to by the acronym, "CNA." Please note the word, "Certified."

A CNA undergoes a course to train him or her in basic patient care, and is licensed to perform her duties.

This includes going to the toilet, with help as needed. It also means assisting the patient with showers.

The CNA helps the patient prepare for bed and sees that he or she is comfortably settled for the night. He or she also helps the patient in starting the day, with whatever degree of assistance may be needed. The CNA assists the nurse, and the resident, with a myriad of details in nursing home life. This may involve meeting requests for appropriate personal favors, time permitting.

By now you should be realizing that in a reputable, highly regarded facility, a team of professionals is at your service. All of them are technically qualified for their jobs. We shall get into personal aspects in a moment.

At this point, we must pause to see where we are in learning our strategy for survival in the nursing home. This is, after all, supposed to be a Nursing Home Survival Guide. Remember, we are seeking survival of our "personhood," of our essential nature as a particular individual.

Hopefully, you will have at least made two entries in that little notebook of yours, regarding essential steps on your road to survival as your essential person.

Those entries would be:
Step No. 1 - Acceptance of My New Reality.
Step No. 2 - Acceptance of My New Roommate.

If you are among the fortunate few to gain a private room, by whatever means, you would of course skip Step No. 2.

We now turn to the next step:

NOTES

Step No. 3 - Interacting With My Caregivers

Here we enter into murky territory, a land of limitless possibilities. I shall offer some general guidelines, and hopefully some specific examples, without even coming close to suggesting some specific individuals you may encounter.

Off we go: Continue to be yourself, but know from the beginning that you should exercise a lot of self-discipline, particularly in early days.

Different people react to different words and different

situations in different ways. Well, yes, we have used the word "different" four times in one sentence, but to make a point.

You will be meeting a number of individuals in a very short time, and self-discipline will enable you to cope with a lot of varying personalities.

As you get to know people, you will find yourself able to relax a bit. You will at some point discover that you prefer some of your caregivers over others. Surprise, friends, surprise, for here we have a microcosm of life in what we may come to think of as the outside world.

Every day, I mean, every day, you will encounter nurses, either LPNs or RNs. On each and every day you will also see CNAs.

Note this: Both nurses and CNAs will have interpersonal skills, that is to say skills in dealing with people. They will also have clinical {nurses} and job {CNAs} skills. Skill levels, you will find, in one area will not necessarily match those in the other.

This is a fancy way of saying that a nurse may be highly competent in clinical skills, but when it comes to relating to people, have all the ability of a clogged sewer line. Oh my, that's a crude way of putting it. I shall try to regain a higher level for the rest of this writing.

The "hall nurse" will be assigned to your section of a hall, or corridor. She will dispense medications, monitor patients' conditions, and respond to CNAs' requests for assistance.

If you are scheduled to receive certain medications within a specified time period, you will receive it. If you have a skin condition of concern, she will monitor it and advise the house physician if she perceives his attention as needed. In some sense, her duties may be limitless. Hers is a serious responsibility.

As you come to know more and more nurses and CNAs, some will become obvious favorites. There will be times when you should do your bit to recognize these folks, a subject we'll get to a bit later.

Others you will tolerate without great effort although you may not especially like them. Finally, there will be some you will positively dislike, and with good reason.

Here is the question: How do

you deal with the latter people, those to whom "with good reason" applies? There is another question: When a caregiver has provided exemplary service, consistently over a period of time, what actions on your part are appropriate? Once again, we find another use for your little notebook.

We will begin with the negative experience. Afterward, we will turn to the positive side.

Let's say a certain nurse has been particularly rude to you. As soon as she is out of sight, take out that little notebook and jot down quotes as best you can remember them. Mark also the time and date.

The sooner you do this, the better, because by attending to the matter promptly, you are more likely to be accurate in recording quotes of that person's remarks. Note also anything relevant you may have said.

Here's another point: Part of the offending person's rudeness may simply have been a refusal to discuss a matter with you. That aspect should be recorded in your notes.

When you have enough

information on hand, it is time to make your request to the Director of Nursing. Write her a note, or given the opportunity, speak briefly to the Director, requesting a few minutes of her time.

As events happen, you may wind up meeting with the Director of Nursing {the "DON"} in her office, or in your room if a private one. Given that names will be mentioned, neither of you will want other ears to overhear.

It may be that if additional conferences are necessary, the Director of Nursing will bring in the Assistant Director of

Nursing or the Welfare Worker. You should have absolute confidence that your privacy and confidentiality will be respected.

It may be that you will have matters to discuss with the DON which involve matters other than personnel issues. My own opinion is that, whatever the matter under discussion, the issue will be resolved in a satisfactory manner.

The outcome of your meetings may not be what you had hoped for or expected. Think about it, especially if you have been harboring some anger, before expressing a dislike for the solution.

Your efforts to recognize exemplary performance will follow an essentially parallel path. In plain English, superb caregiving will also be most effectively reported if you document performance as you did negative work.

Yes, it's once again time to get out that little notebook. Over a period of time, document incidents, being careful to note details. By that I mean date, time, what is said, and the circumstances surrounding the incident. When you have enough information, after considerable thought, to make your case, write a note to the Director of Nursing. Have that note delivered to her office by a person whom you have every reason to trust; that is every reason to believe she will actually make the delivery, while confirming that she has made it.

Kindly note that the gender pronoun, "she," is used more often than "he." Such use reflects the realities of nursing home staffing. Men as well as women serve as competent nurses and CNAs. The intention here is not to suggest otherwise.

You will note I am expressing somewhat positive views concerning resolution of issues where the Director of Nursing is involved. I shall say only that my positive outlook is based on personal experience.

My own view is that the Director of Nursing may be your best friend in the facility in which you live.

For the while, lets "eliminate the negative and accent the positive," as the old Johnny Mercer song would have it. You do remember Johnny Mercer, don't you?

Never mind, we move on to

other and positive matters. That is to say, we shall now discuss ways to enhance your relationships with those who care for you.

Accentuating the Positive

These days it is the negative that seems to get the most attention. Shootings, robberies, corruption, even assault and rape, and so on. There is the joking line about television newscasts and newspaper front pages, "If it bleeds, it leads." Here's a little secret: If you accentuate the positive in a sincere, and I mean sincere, way, it will make a difference in your nursing facility life.

You should, yes, you should, feel genuine respect and gratitude for and toward those who provide your care. You should tell them so often, but not so often your remarks begin to have a phony ring.

It is still true that "Please" and "Thank You" have a remarkable effect on those who provide the services on which you depend.

If these folks feel enthusiastically about you, their patient, as a human being, it will make a difference. Where individuals are concerned with whom you develop a special empathy, you will enjoy each other's company. Because you will spend the most time with CNAs, it is with them that such a situation is most likely to happen.

Have friends or family provided you with soda, candy or other treats? Offer to share them. Now the offer may be declined because of a lack of desire, or a feeling that the employer might not approve. Whatever the reason, trust me, the offer will be appreciated.

If, for example, you have become friends with a

particular CNA, as times goes by you will likely learn something of her personal life. Having learned something of her family, her hobbies, or her dog, you should ask about them.

Now friends, much of the above will seem, and be, elementary, especially if you have learned to relate to people in an effective way. If not, here's a chance to further your personal development. It is never too late to concentrate on this area of living.

A Word of Caution: It is quite possible, even probable, that you will encounter in at least one caregiver some very irritating traits. There may be only one.

I speak here of irritating traits concerning which you will be able to do absolutely nothing. You will simply have to tolerate the situation, presenting your most pleasant possible face.

Of negative traits, the ones that annoy me most are vigorously chewing gum and horrible misuse of the English language. Such phrases as "I don't ..." or "I didn't want none ... {the classic double negative} drive me up the proverbial wall. Yet I have learned to put on the best possible face, and to accept the situation as one I cannot change. Well, enough of that!

We have discussed handling or managing the positive and the negative in terms of interaction with your caregivers. There is of course no possible way to predict or discuss every situation in which you may find yourself. Likewise, there is no possibly way to cover all of life's solutions.

But you should at least by now have an idea of the kind of experiences you may expect, and how to deal with many of them.

Now, lets get out that little notebook. Again, I ask: trust me. Keep drumming the essentials into your mind.

Tip: At least for a time, look at that notebook again and again. In it, by this point you should see, at a very minimum those key steps. Hopefully, you will also have made notes to help you along your way.

Perhaps we are oversimplifying here, but it all should be subsumed under those key steps. "Subsume" is a fancy word meaning "grouped under."

And now {drum roll please}

here again are those key steps which should absolutely be in your little note book:

Step No. 1 - Acceptance of My New Reality

Step No. 2 - Acceptance of My New Roommate

{Unless of course you are fortunate enough to have a private room}

Step No. 3 - Interacting With My Caregivers

We are not through yet on our road to Survival of Your Personhood. "Personhood" is another fancy term, in this case one which means "individual identity." This is a time to think about not only preserving the essential You, but to change any – how shall we say this? – aspects of you that might stand improving. That is, just in case there are any.

And so it is that we have arrived at next step:

NOTES

Step No. 4 - Preserving My Identity.

Let it first be noted that even in a semi-private room you will have a little space at your disposal.

This is space, given reasonable limits, which you may use as you wish. There should be a connection for your TV set. And there should be some storage or shelf space. Use this apace for your identity preservation. Here one speaks seriously.

Whatever your interests have been, you may be able to continue them. If you are a stamp collector, you probably won't have room for all of your collection. But you should be able to bring some of it, quite likely the part or parts most important to you.

There is no possible way to cover all questions a nursing home applicant may have, or to discuss ways to continue them. Still, you should look for ways, and for space. Remember that these interests are a large part of what you have become as a person.

Have you used a computer? Here's hoping so, because the doors a computer opens in terms of making and maintaining friendships, and of developing new interests, are limitless.

I have been very fortunate in living in a facility in which a supportive management has provided a wireless Internet connection. Because I have a private room, management has supported the building of a large-scale model railway.

It is limited in length, to be sure, but it still provides endless hours of pleasure, because of generosity of spirit on the part of the friend building it, and the equal important support of facility management.

Please note: This pleasure does much to make my nursing home living palatable.

Before ending this little essay, we will devote another step to personal security. At the moment, it is appropriate to address computer security.

If you have a computer in a nursing facility, put a password on it. I shall repeat: Put a password on your computer. This is important whether you live in a semi-private room, as is likely, or in a private one.

As time goes by, you will in all probability have more and

more sensitive and personal information in your computer. If you don't know how to enter a password into your computer, someone known to you or a member of your family should be available to do it for you.

Tip: Turn your computer "off" when you leave the room. If you leave it "on" in your absence, anyone, that is anyone, can access any information in your computer. You just don't want that to happen do you? Remember the axiom, "My business is my business."

In sum, bring as many of your

interests and passions with you as possible. At the same time, remember that there is a limit, which will probably seem severe to you at the time.

In all likelihood you will be asking friends and family to hold on to your stuff. Ask for their cooperation, as you explain that it will take a bit of time to decide what you want to keep, and what you will authorize to be discarded. Some items may fall into the category of "Why in the world have I held on to "this" for so long?

In a real way, your interests are your essence. Think about

what we've been discussing. Those thoughts should be of considerable help in focusing on the matter at hand.

There is one final step to be considered. After we discuss it, we will again list all the steps to be kept in mind, and then you will be on your own.

There is one final step to be considered. Remember that, although we have listed steps in a sequential fashion, you will be dealing with more than one step at a time.

In effect, depending on rapidly changing circumstances, you will be dealing with all of them in a simultaneous fashion.

And now {another drum roll, please}, here is our last step:

NOTES

Step No. 5 - Personal Security

The steps we now propose will eventually seem obvious. Please remember, many, if not most, of your facility's occupants will be persons of diminished mental acuity. This condition will of course vary in degree from individual to individual.

First and foremost, put your name on everything possible. With many items, labels are the neatest and most convenient answer, all the more so if you have a computer and printer.

For the purpose of computer-printer labeling, I recommend Avery Label # 8160, available at any good office supply store. By mentioning a specific label product, we are hopefully saving you a lot of time-consuming shopping around.

For clothing, you will need a Sharpie pen, or some other writing instrument which can be used on clothing. While clothing may be an unlikely item for stealing, having your name on clothing items can make a difference in the laundry getting your clothing back to you and not to another person.

If the laundry returns an item and your name is not on it as you prepare to dress, the item may belong to someone else.

Please note this caution: Do not, to repeat, do not, leave cash in your room.

If you simply must keep small amounts, keep it hidden in a place which, for the unknowing, would probably be very difficult to find.

For most amounts, simply request your business office to establish a personal account in your name. Your family will be able to make deposits to it, and you will, as needed, be able to make withdrawals. This is by far the better and safest way to handle cash.

As to other valuable items, whatever they may be, don't just leave them lying around in plain view. Use what we all understand when we say "common sense."

You will not be accustomed to thinking in security terms, at least to such a degree, when you enter your facility. You need not think of security matters every minute of every hour, once you have established these habits and practices.

Please remember: In the beginning, you should "think security."

NOTES

Chapter Three - Summing Up

By now we have covered a lot of ground. I'm thinking of you as a friend, though we will probably never meet. This is because you will be treading the same ground as I have, and as I continue to do.

More and more in this writing, I have found myself
thinking: "I wish someone had told me all of these things in the beginning, that I had been given access to these words and pages." So I am particularly anxious that all of this is helpful to you.

The wisdom of keeping a little

notebook has been mentioned more than once. It need not necessarily be "little," but it should be kept conveniently at hand. If something seems interesting at the time and later proves a bit less so, it may still be useful in forming your overall impressions.

Now, no matter how your organize your notebook for the most part, it will probably be of great help to list the five steps on a separate page at the very beginning.

Once again, here they are:

The Five Steps

Step No. 1 - Acceptance of My

New Reality

Step No. 2 - Acceptance of My New Roommate

{Unless of course you have a private room}

Step No. 3 - Interacting With My Caregivers

Step No. 4 - Preserving My Identity

Step No. 5 - Personal Security

And there you have it, except for a final few words of caution. These have to do with procedures and practices to which you may have some difficulties in becoming accustomed.

By the way, it is presumed that if you are reading these words on your own behalf, your mental acuity is, for all intents and purposes, functioning well. If you are a family member reading here on behalf of a less fortunate person, you may have to interpret them in a particularly individual way.

All of the above being said, when your CNA inquires politely as to your intended bedtime, this will be something new. Chances are you have not had to ponder the matter much in advance, and especially not having to advise another person.

If staff is functioning properly, you will be asked for meal preferences for mid-day and evening meals, by whatever name they are called.

Depending on your condition or situation, you may feel that if someone comes around to take your vital signs {temperature and blood pressure} just one more time in a day, you will want to scream.

Try to be nice. Remember, As mentioned earlier, these things are being performed in your best interest. Trust me.

A CNA will be present in assisting you to get up, dress, and start your day. Ditto in reverse at bedtime. A "Sit

Stand" device may be required to actually carry you at these times.

Yes, sometimes having to have such help is demeaning. It may be of a little comfort to imagine how you would manage without all of this assistance.

Don't worry about keeping up with your weight. Another person will likely see to it, depending on medical orders.

At some point you may realize an essential truth: You are here because your own physical limitations, your own medical needs, require it. This is a no-fault situation. It is not your fault, the fault of your caregivers, or the fault of your family. If you have a loving family, be grateful for each member, and let them know it.

Does anyone ever tire of hearing "Please" or "Thank You" or "I Love You?" The answer is no, they don't.

Hopefully you will have been given these words to read before, or as you begin, your journey of living in a nursing home environment. I truly hope they will be of assistance to you now and in coming days

A Final Reminder: Keep that notebook, and use it.

And now, I wish you good journey the maximum of success, and even ***Moments of Joy*** in your new environment.

Remember, Dear Sir or Mam, you can do it. **YOU CAN**.

With all good wishes from your fellow traveler,

Sincerely,

A. Frank Rushton, PhD

Nursing Home Resident

NOTES

NOTES

NOTES

About the Author:

Frank Rushton spent the majority of his career at the ETV Branch of the U.S. Army Aviation Center where, as a civilian, he was employed for twenty-five years as a Television Writer-Director. Prior to that, he had worked for a number of years as a staff director at Atlanta, Georgia, television stations.

In the past, his interests have included photography of prototype railroads. He now enjoys an unusual large scale model railway, which he and a friend, John Andrews, designed, and which Mr. Andrews is building for him. On the Internet, he pursues interests in British railways and in the study of reptiles. Dr. Rushton is now a permanent resident in a nursing home.

He holds an ABJ {Bachelor of Arts in Journalism} from the Henry W. Grady School of Journalism, University of Georgia; an MS degree {Foundations of Education} from Troy State University at Fort Rucker; and a PhD {Instructional Systems} from the Center for Educational Technology, Florida State University, Tallahassee.

Alternative Book Press is a publishing company with many new and exciting books coming out. visit www.alternativebookpress.com and sign up to receive emails and deals today!

www.ingramcontent.com/pod-product-compliance
Lightning Source LLC
Chambersburg PA
CBHW052135270326
41930CB00012B/2895